GO FOR IT

Matthew Martino

ISBN: **1489520430**
ISBN-13: **978-1489520432**

DEDICATION

I would like to dedicate this book to my mother Beauty Chihwai , who has for most of her life been involved in a business of some sort. She has always coached me on the importance and advantage of working for yourself.

I would also like to thank TJ Lyons for taking time out of his busy schedule to compile some information for this book in as well as endorsing it.

CONTENTS

This book started writing itself way back in 2011. I had quit my job and started a one-man consultancy service. I immediately got my first client – in fact, even before I was released from my previous job. As I went along, many questions started popping up. I have no family background in business and had to turn to books and the Internet to find answers. I spent thousands of pounds on buying books (and then reading them), hundreds of hours browsing the internet, subscribing to blogs, reading posts, searching for answers. I downloaded books and papers from the internet and studied them. I took notes, did exercises, and did a lot of writing to clarify concepts to myself. I could see some light. Whenever introduced to anybody doing business – any kind of business – I would ask him questions. In the beginning I did not even know what questions to ask and how to ask them.

Then my consultancy failed. After the initial shock and sulking, after the deeply hurt ego recovered a bit, I again sat down and wrote out all the mistakes I made – not a confession, nor self-whipping, nor did I play the blame game. I tried to be as objective as possible.

One part of my personality deeply feels for others. It prompts me to be a Good Samaritan. I reasoned that there are several technically qualified professionals rendering professional services. They will also make the same or similar mistakes and I must rescue them.

A young man started an Internet Café close to where I was staying. I used to visit his café for scanning and printing work. A posh 16-cubicle air-conditioned café on the ground floor but hardly any surfers. I could see that he was doing all the wrong things and not doing any of the right things. The rescuer in me woke up and started advising him. But he was overly confident about managing his business as I was a first year Degree of Business student, He argued with me on all points and rejected them. This went on for some three four months. Then his Café closed down. We did not meet even to say goodbye.

It was painful to see the business going down the drain. Many times I wished I had never met him. Although I was an unintended beneficiary of his business. His business was a live case study for me.

This whole episode compelled me do a lot of concrete thinking and helped me validate several of the concepts and models I had read about.

Years passed.

One day, on the 11th October, 2012, to be precise, while taking a stock count at my book distribution center, I decided to write a book for such starters.

Next time I see someone on the path the Internet Café owner walked, the rescuer in me will again try to tell him a thing or two. But he will debate with me and reject my advice. Then I'll say —Look here, I am some kind of an expert on this. I even wrote a book on this subject and hope that his business is saved.

1. HOW TO READ THIS BOOK ?

Good question. I'm glad you asked. Shows your thorough nature. I like that.

One answer, and most useful is 'wisely'.

Which means following the points below

- Make time to read the book.

- Buy a notebook with several pages for notes.

- Gather together a number of colored pens. Also include blue and black..

- Take those earplugs off and switch off the mobile and the TV.

- Start reading from the cover page. Keep a pen in hand.

- Read with the assumption that it is meant for your benefit.

- Read the book as a workbook, not a novel.

- As you read, keep asking yourself, —How can I use this for my business? ‖

- As you read further, a number of thoughts and questions will crop up in your mind.

- Write your responses to those questions, take note of those thoughts and unanswered questions in the margin of the book or in the note book and you will find the answer as you read through.

- Underline any sentence you feel is important. Give it more thought. Write down your responses.

- If you disagree with something I say, note it down and write in red ink —I don't agree with this. Then, in blue or black ink write why you disagree and what your view is.

- Simultaneously, keep jotting points and ideas you liked. This is important.

2. Assumptions about You

There are a few assumptions I am making while writing this book. This I am doing for facilitating the process of writing and maintaining a certain focus. I am aware that this is artificial. I am very well aware that not all of these assumptions will apply to you. That, however will not in any way affect the applicability of the principles we will be discussing. They are universal.

The first assumption I am making is that you are very young or in college or university or just trying to find your path.

The second assumption I am making is that you like every typical aspiring entrepreneur have a laptop and mobile phone.

My third assumption is that now that you have finished your studies or are just about to there is pressure on you to be on your own and start earning.

The fourth assumption I make is that you are currently in the process of deciding what you will do for earning your livelihood.

My fifth assumption is that there is no business background in your family or relatives or acquaintances. So if you decide to start your own business you will be the first one in your family to do so, what is technically called the first generation entrepreneur.

A corollary of the fifth assumption is that you are unlikely to get business guidance within the family. This is my sixth assumption.

The seventh one is that although you have appeared or will appear for university recruitment meetings, you are open about considering other options available for earning a livelihood.

My eighth assumption is that whatever the mode of earning the livelihood, you wish to put your technical knowledge and skills to use for this purpose.

My ninth assumption is that although you did think about striking on your own, you felt a bit uncomfortable about it, because what information you had was not enough and what you heard from others was not very encouraging.

My tenth assumption is that your friends are also similarly placed about the above assumptions and especially about the tenth one.

I further assume that you are intelligent, quick to learn new things and concepts, are a methodical worker and a hard-working person. I also assume that you have such qualities as perseverance, honesty, straightforwardness, caring, dependability, trustworthiness. I assume that you are enthusiastic, quick to act and do not put things off and that you are action-oriented.

I am very certain that you do have these qualities, don't worry even if you think you don't. Later on we will have a look at some of the qualities that you will need to hone in for better results.

3. Do Not Feel Guilty, If You Desire to be Rich

Each and every one of us wants to be rich. We have always wanted to be. But the middle-class philosophy has always acted as a barrier to openly talk about it and try to achieve that goal. The middle-class as a whole says: Simple Living and High Thinking. So the underlying suggestion is, don't be rich. Be middle-class. There are several arguments put forth in support of not becoming wealthy.

I do not wish to go into them: all of them are illogical and hold no substance. What I will instead do is just illustrate to you that earning riches has always been supported by various religions. That will take care of any feeling of guilt about earning a lot of money that may have been put into you.

4.   Job versus Business: Why Choose to do Business?

What is the one concern that is uppermost in your mind as you finish your studies and step out in the world? I guess your answer is getting a job'. If it is, pause for a moment. Think. What is it exactly that you want? A job? Are you sure? Think again. Why do you want a job? Do you love a job? Do you love some organization and want to work there? What do you want to do with a job? What do you think you will achieve if you get a job?

You don't love a corporation. You want a job to earn money. To pay off the education loan. To buy essential and luxury items. What you will achieve through a job is a means of earning livelihood. It is not the job that you love.

Then why aren't we saying - I want to start earning money instead of saying - I want a job?‖

This is because in our minds earning a living has become synonymous with a job. Like it happened with Xerox. Xeroxing has become so synonymous with photocopying that we have forgotten the original word. We have come to think that a job is the only means of earning living.

But need it be so? Are there no options available to us? Of course there are, if we care to consider them. One option is doing a business. On the face of it most of you may not like the idea. But I invite you to make an informed choice. It does not matter if you opt for service. That's fine. But it should only be after considering the alternatives to doing a job. The decision should be taken after taking the pros and cons of both, a job and a business.

To help you in making an informed decision, here is a small comparison of both. Please study it.

What's good about a job:

- Immediate earning, every month

- Constant flow of money, no ups and downs

- Annual raises

- Possibilities for promotions

- Title, social status

- PF, pension, perquisites

- Retirement benefits

- Few risks

What's not so good about a job:

- Tough to get

- Salary remains within a band

- Raises are small

- A major chunk goes for paying income tax (3 – 4 months' salary)

- Cut-throat competition – rat race

- No choice about nature of work, colleagues or bosses

- Tremendous work pressure

- Work / project may not be to your liking

- Illusive job security

- Office politics, prejudices

- Worry about your organization

- Maybe, no job satisfaction

All these factors are beyond your control. You can't do anything about any of them.

What's good about doing your own business?

You are the BOSS

What does it mean?

- You decide what kind of work you'll do.

- You decide with whom you will work.

- You decide whether to take up a project or not.

- You decide who your assistants will be.

- You decide the priorities.

- You decide what's important.

- You decide the vision and the mission.

- You decide the goals and the budget.

- You decide the strategies and the tactics.

- You decide salaries and working hours.

- You decide what assets to buy.

- You decide what work to do in house and what to outsource.

- You decide how much to expand.

- You decide where and when to divert, how much and how long.

- You monitor.

- You don't take orders, you issue orders.

- You don't get hired, you hire.

- You don't get fired, you fire, if necessary.

- You don't get promoted, you promote.

- You don't implement someone else's ideas, your ideas get implemented.

- You don't obey someone else's orders, your orders get obeyed.

- Someone else doesn't decide your title; you decide your own title.

- You decide when to become aggressive and when to lie low, go slow.

- You don't live someone else's script, you write your own script.

- Your life is not controlled by someone else, you decide for yourself.

- You don't have to look elsewhere for job security, you are the job security.

- You do exactly the work you like and say no to what you don't. Naturally you feel happy doing that work and satisfied when it is done. Your work is never boring to you.

- Better chances of building assets

You have better chances of building assets as you first incur expenditure and pay taxes on what remains. In a job you first pay taxes and then spend and (try to) save from whatever remains. Very little remains.

5.   Feeling of pride

You create business from scratch with imagination and hard work. You see it grow from a small idea into a robust entity. That gives you a great feeling of pride. This is completely missing in a job. You get to opportunities for building relationships and networking. You make contacts and associate with a lot of more people. You help them and they help you, even your competitors. This is much more a helpful network than that of colleagues and bosses.

Ease of starting

It is very easy to start a service venture. All you need is a laptop, a mobile phone, an Internet connection, a vehicle, business cards and some sundry stationery, a sweet tongue, a cool head, and determination to make it. Most of the things required to do business are in your head or you can learn. You don't need a posh office, nor a fancy address. You can start from home, no; you can start from your study room. If you can manage to have a website of your own, great! You don't need much capital to start with, although you will need financial support for a few months till your venture takes off.

What's not so good about starting your business:
The buck stops with you. You have to take all decisions. Decision making is stressful. A wrong decision can harm the business. Discipline. You are the boss. If you do not have self-discipline, there can be problems.

Too much to do. Product development, purchases, production, dispatch, billing, follow up, collection, banking, legal matters, accounting, marketing, selling, networking, planning, monitoring, administration, taxes ...... the list is long.

Competition. Too much and too stiff competition. Difficult for new entrants to survive.

Capital. You just never have enough of it!

Obsolescence. Your product, your technology may go out of fashion. Your

knowledge may become obsolete.

Long hours and long gestation period.

Copycats. Others can copy your product or service and compete with me.

Too many rules, laws and licenses.

No or little support / help

Expert help is costly.

There is no denying that these problems do exist. But contrary to the not-so-good factors of service or a job, there are several ways and remedies to reduce their intensity or sidestep them. And unlike in a job, many of them are under your control

A job is a T shirt of one size. It never fits. It's either too tight or too loose. Its neck is either too small or so large that it makes you feel uncomfortable. Its sleeves are either too tight or loose or too long or short. And, finally, its length , It may cover half of your thighs or end near your waist. And you've got to wear it as it is. You are not, mind you, allowed to alter it in any way. What's the point in wearing such a T shirt just for the sake of a prominent company's logo on the chest (it may actually come on your belly!) on it? Oh! I was forgetting about the colour.

Instead, why not have a T shirt tailored for your height, body-shape, your arm muscles, the colour and the shade of your choice and your company's logo on the front and the back and wear it proudly and happily, and in return, undertake to make it prominent?

Think about it, seriously.

6. What Kinds of Businesses Have a Better Chance of Survival

In the previous chapter, I put before you the positives and negatives of a job and business and invited you to compare them and have a balanced view. I hope you have done this exercise. May be you have taken help of elders in your family and others whose opinions you value.

Now, if, after this exercise you are ready to consider starting your own business, suddenly hundreds of questions will have cropped up in your mind.

So, straight away I will proceed to make your life slightly easier by dealing with your first major concern: If I start a business of my own, what is the guarantee that it will survive? How can I make sure that it does not fail?

Survival of an enterprise is the top most concern of every entrepreneur all the time. Profitability and growth follow, at number two and three. Entrepreneurs are therefore deeply concerned about this aspect when choosing a line of business for their proposed ventures.

In this chapter we will discuss a sociological model of survival of ventures and come up with several recommendations on things to keep in mind while choosing a business or line of activity. This can help entrepreneurs like you make more informed decisions.

All businesses are social systems in as much as they are operated by members of a society, and interact with their environment, which is the society. This interaction is on two levels: social and economic. In this chapter we shall also examine the social interaction and draw actionable and implementable inferences.

The Basic Model of Entrepreneurship

All societies have certain unfulfilled needs because of which its members face problems or difficulties. The magnitude and severity of these unfulfilled needs may vary from small irritants to huge barriers that block the progress of the society. An enterprising person, the entrepreneur, spots these needs and proceeds to fulfil them to the best of his abilities. If his activity satisfies the unfulfilled need of the society, the society supports the activity by buying his product or service, at a price. The venture thus gets established and as the entrepreneur finds running it profitable, he continues the venture. Thus a mutually beneficial relationship gets established between the entrepreneur and the society in which he operates: a win-win situation. This is the basic model of entrepreneurship.

The Model of Survival of Entrepreneurship

So long as the relationship between the society and the entrepreneur remains mutually beneficial, the venture has a potential to survive. This relationship, however, develops over a period. The society has to develop trust in the entrepreneur – a faith in his ability to deliver the
promised solution, the adequacy and effectiveness of the solution and his uprightness and fairness in dealings. Till the society is thus satisfied, the entrepreneur and his business can be said to be on some kind of trial. Those who fail this trial have to close shop. But once this vote of trust is won, harmonious relations develop between the entrepreneur and the society.

This results in development and expansion of a growth spiral. As the entrepreneur's solutions continue to solve the problems of the society, or fulfil its needs, the society benefits and prospers. This in turn results in the growth of the entrepreneur's enterprise. He prospers. His venture expands and offers employment to members of the society which in turn increases the society's purchasing power and overall prosperity of both, the enterprise and the society.

While the above growth spiral is active, a lot of developments keep taking place in the society. A society is always changing, albeit very slowly, imperceptibly. It is never stagnant. There are several factors responsible for this. There are technological developments. There is fresh knowledge and information pouring in. There are economic factors – both positive and negative. There are political factors. And then, there's plain dissatisfaction or boredom with what is available. Many times solving one problem leads to development of another problem – may be at a higher level, and sometimes the solution itself gives rise to unfelt needs.

The society is constantly being impacted by all these and several other factors. The effect of these factors is usually felt over a longish period, slowly. However, on account of these, a solution which may have been perfect when offered, may start proving inadequate or unattractive and gradually lose its utility and therefore favour with the society, even resulting in the entrepreneur's going out of business.

Takeaways:

If you are an entrepreneur scouting for a suitable venture, the simple model discussed above offers you at least fifteen takeaways to help you make more informed decisions. Here they are:

1. Your venture must solve a problem for the society or fulfil a need.

Corollary 1: The more basic the need or the problem, the better the chances of survival of your business.

Corollary 2: The more severe or urgent the problem, the better.

Corollary 3: The broader the constituencies whose needs you are planning to meet or problem you propose to solve, the better.

Corollary 4: The more scalable the business, the better.

Corollary 5: The longer lasting the need, the better.

Corollary 6: One product, solution or service may not be sufficient, or may not find favour with the potential users. You must therefore have more than one product to start with.

2. You must have the capacity to solve the problem or fulfill the

need. That is, either you yourself have to have the technical knowledge / domain knowledge or hire somebody who has.

Corollary : You must have a passion for what you are proposing to do, otherwise you may not succeed, or, even if you do succeed, it will be a hollow success.

3. Your solution must actually solve the problem or fulfil the need.

4. Your charges or fees should be such that a majority of the members of the society should find it worth it.

5. You must be honest, ethical, trustworthy and fair to deal with. This is very fundamental. All your dealings and actions must constantly demonstrate these qualities.

Corollary: You must have a strong network in the community. For success in business, it is extremely important as to how many people know you in a favourable way, for they are the ones who are likely to recommend you to others.

6. Once your business is established and starts growing, you must start and keep contributing to the betterment of your society. You must give back and keep giving back and participate in the growth and development of the society by creating employment opportunities and through charity.

Corollary: You must pass on the benefits of expanding scale of operations to your customers by improving your solution, lowering your prices etc.

7. Through your interactions with your supporters, customers, non-customers, socially and politically active members of the society and so on and through other information media, you must keep studying the changing trends in the economy in general and your field in particular and plan how you will respond to these changes on the horizon so that your business does not become obsolete, ie: you must innovate constantly.

The above is not a complete list of conditions for survival of a venture. This is an outcome only of examining the social perspective. The entrepreneur will need to take into account preconditions arising out of other perspectives such as economic, business management, financial management and marketing.

The knowledge of what kinds of businesses have a better chance of survival and prospering, from the sociological point of view will be very helpful to you in choosing your line. But your business idea will also need to pass some other tests, which we will discuss in a later chapter.
But right now let us have a look at what moral obligations you, the entrepreneur have towards your customers.

Moral Obligation to Customers

By virtue of starting an enterprise or a venture, an entrepreneur comes under various kinds of obligations to various entities in the society. Some of these obligations are legal and can be enforced by the law enforcing agencies, if necessary. Some are financial obligations and the lenders can enforce them as per the agreement or the law. Some obligations are social in nature, and although they may be nebulous and fuzzy in nature, and may or may not be legally enforceable, society has its own mechanism to enforce them. And finally some obligations are moral in nature. It is these obligations that we will look into in this article.

Every entrepreneur has legal, financial, social and moral obligations towards his customers / clients. While the former three operate at the gross level, the moral obligations operate at much higher a level. In case of legal, social and financial obligations, there are external agencies that can compel or extract performance from the entrepreneur. But in case of moral obligations, there are no external agencies. There are no taskmasters, no prosecutor, and no enactments to go by and there are no penalties, so to say, to be paid. Here the observer and the one being observed are one and the same persons.

Justification of actions is to be given, not to the judge or the income tax authorities, but to one's own conscience. One has to judge oneself in one's own eyes. Have I failed in my own eyes? is the question one has to answer to oneself.

The moral obligations that rest on your shoulders as an entrepreneur are because of your superior capacities and capabilities that your customer / client has put his faith in. It is always so in fairer, civilized societies. The more powerful a person the more obligations he has.

Your obligation is to actually remove the pain felt by your customer / client that you promised you will remove. Your obligation is to actually solve a problem faced by your customer / client that you claim you can solve and because of this claim the customer / client came to you.

Your obligation is to give him your attention and carry on the transaction with care and concern, with personal involvement – to his satisfaction. In the field of administration of justice, there is a famous maxim – justice not only must be done, but must also appear to have been done. Similarly, not only must excellent service be rendered to the customer / client, he must also experience that you have given him excellent service. Even if you are only a seller or supplier of goods, it is your obligation to be familiar with its use or working and guide the customer if he so desires.

Your obligation is to always keep your technical knowledge up to date and put it at the service of your customer / client. That's what he is paying you for.

In sum, your moral responsibility is to be just and fair to your customer / client, not to dupe, deceive or defraud him by giving him substandard service or goods or shortchanging him in any ways, even if he is never likely to discover it. And how do you know you have discharged your moral obligation well? Simple.

What happens when you later recall the incidence / transaction? Do you feel guilty? Does your conscience pinch you? Do you feel disturbed? Or does a small smile beautify your face as the pleased face of the satisfied customer appears before your mind's eye?

I told you there's no external judge here!

7. Clarify Your Purpose

In the previous two chapters, we have dealt with two very important aspects of doing a business, namely, fulfilling a need or solving a problem, or making things easy and how to give your venture a moral base, which will be spotted by your customers and they will love it. Now we go a step further and clarify to ourselves why we want to do this business. This exercise gives you a focus. It, among other things, helps you decide what fits and what doesn't fit in your purpose which makes decision making, saying 'Yes or No' easier and based on specific criteria, not haphazardly.

Before you start your business, even before you start taking steps and making preparations, it is necessary to clarify to yourself why you want to go into a business.

Obviously you want to earn profit for yourself and you believe that doing this business will help. You need to go deeper into this. Why? Because this fundamental thinking will have a long term impact on all your decisions and actions. In a way it will define the scope of your business.

So start by asking yourself this question:

If profit were not the issue, would I still do this business? And if I would, why would I?

As usual, write this question in your notebook and write answers. Build up your list of answers over a time. Believe me, this will be a great help. In a short space, it gives you your mission and vision!
The answer to this question will reveal your liking for the field you are choosing.

See, doing a business because you know the technical stuff of the business is one thing and doing it because you love it, you are passionate about it, because you sincerely believe that other players in the field are not doing it right and therefore the customers are suffering, that you can do it better and that will give more value to the customer / user is totally different. It takes your business to an entirely different plane.

If you go into a business only because you know how to do it, you will do it as a job. This defeats the most important purpose of doing your own business – to enjoy it. If you go into a business only because you know how to do it, you will not have any incentive to update your knowledge. You will keep doing the same things in the same way year in and year out, that is, until someone with current, up to date knowledge sets up a shop down the road. That will mean the end of the road for your venture.

If you are doing it only for the sake of making profit, it is only money that you will focus on, value to the customer will be only a secondary consideration.

If you are doing it only for the sake of profit, sterling quality work will be out of the question. You will tend to use substandard, cheap material, employ workers who work shoddily because they are cheap, and render no or minimal and poor
after-sales service to cut on expenses. How long do you think your customers will stay with you? Can you reasonably expect them to recommend you to others?

If you are doing it only for the sake of making money, you will abandon it the moment financial equations of the business change adversely. What happens to the customers will be of no concern to you. And you will go into some other business that is more paying at the moment. But your reputation will follow you.

Can you guess what will happen in the long term?

As a matter of fact, you cannot do business only for the sake of profit. Profit is the by-product that comes out of serving your customers.

Profit is a by-product that comes out of solving some problem that your customers are facing.

Profit is a by-product of the process of removing or reducing some pain or inconvenience your customers face. But, if money is not your sole concern, you are liberated. You become free to focus on the client's needs and satisfying him by giving him the greatest value you can. You will stretch yourself happily to solve his problem. You will regularly spend time updating your knowledge. You will constantly search new methods and techniques to improve your products, using fresh knowledge; fresh insights gained by your experience and research taking place in your field. That will benefit your customers who will become your fans and wholeheartedly and enthusiastically recommend you to others.

There is another point you need to consider while clarifying your purpose.Is your idea of a business for you that it will help you have a decent lifestyle like free evenings, a full weekly off and at least a fortnight of annual holiday? Does your picture of your business start and end with you? Will you continue in the business so long as you can and then either sell it or just close it down and retire?

Or your vision extends to creating something that will outlive you, that you will hand it over to your son or daughter, who, in turn will pass it on to your grand children ?

There is nothing wrong or right about any of the choices. It is absolutely fine. But the point is being aware. Being aware of your intentions is essential because that will decide the kind of business you choose and the foundation you will need to lay.

You may find it difficult to do this thinking because it needs you to peep too deep in to the future. And future, even near future is difficult to visualize. But persist. I assure you, doing this exercise will give you considerable maturity about looking at things. I have seen this happen.

If you find this a difficult thing to do, I suggest that you discuss this with other business owners. Look around and you will find businesses responding to both the above criteria. Befriend them and ask them. Don't be shy. They will be glad to help.

Exercise

Ask yourself these questions:

- What am I trying to achieve through my business?

Write down this question on a fresh page in your notebook and try and write as many answers to it as you can come up with. Don't be shy of writing even silly sounding replies like 'having fun', 'making others jealous of me', 'avoid working for some other idiot', etc. The more answers you come up with, the better. As usually happens with such exercises, fresh reasons may occur to you later, when you are doing something else. Keep adding. This will help you clarify your purpose and the objective of doing this business. Share them with your family and friends.

- What do I expect from my business? Lifestyle or legacy?

As above write your answers. Stick with it even if it takes a few days. One need not hurry about fundamental thinking.

You should at least one idea on which you base your business. Maybe you have more. Let's now take that or those ideas and examine them. They must pass some tests before we tie ourselves with it.

8.   Examine Your Business Idea

Now let's talk about the business idea. It is well and good that you have a great idea. But will it work? Your idea has a better chance of gaining market acceptance if it does at least some of the following things:

☐ Make something difficult easy, or,

☐ Make something expensive cheap, or,

☐ Make something that entertains

☐ Eases a great pain of at least a segment of people (it is better to make a small number of customers extremely happy than make a large number of people marginally happy. When this happens, word quickly spreads and customers seek you out.)

☐ Also you should pick up and idea where you can empathize with your users. Then you are better able to understand their pain and work with full dedication to solve it.

☐ You need to be passionate about it. This is necessary, once again, to ensure working with full dedication and involvement, superior quality of solutions, and sustaining you through rough times.

☐ The idea must be scalable, i. e. it must be possible to do it on a large scale. This is necessary so that expanding your business becomes easy.

Exercise

- Look at your idea. How many and which of the above criteria does it fulfil?

Now the question is, should your idea be original, something new, never tried before? Relax. Don't get stressed. This is not necessary. An idea which someone else has already used for business can be good enough. In fact, it is much easier to succeed with an old idea, because it is already established. People have a fair idea of what it is, what to expect from it, how it works etc.

So, you do not have to educate people or create a demand. The demand is already there. You only need to fulfill it. But if your idea is brand new, something that has never been done before, a lot of ground work by way of educating the market and creating a demand will have to be done. This needs money, time and effort. So to that extent your costs go up. And then just about when you have created the market and are ready to reap the profits, your competitor steps in and starts the business - at much lower costs! So, do not try to be a pioneer or path breaker. Take up an idea which already has a market for and get into it, without any hesitation or feeling guilty.

Try out your original idea later when you are well established and your customers start trusting you.

However, a carbon or Xerox copy of an existing business will not work. The market has no place for duplicates. There has to be something to differentiate your product or service from the other similar ones. Criteria already discussed above will apply.

While on the topic of ideas here are a few more points:

Ideas are relatively worthless. They are cheaper by the dozen. Only when backed by a solid business plan and competent team to execute them, do they become useful business ideas.

Ideas evaporate very quickly. Ideas strike us and after a few hours or so we completely forget them. It is therefore necessary to capture and note ideas as soon as they occur to us. Therefore, always carry a diary or a notebook wherever you go so that no ideas escape.

Note ideas in some details. Cryptic or one word description will not make any sense after a few days. An enterprise cannot survive for long on one single business idea. There are at least two dangers. One is the danger of obsolescence and the other is the danger of being copied. You must therefore always have at least two or three ideas up your sleeve.

Ideas have a definite life of their own and unless modified or fortified, will stop being profitable.
One need not wait for ideas to strike or occur. There are a number of techniques like brainstorming to generate ideas.

Success or failure of an idea depends much on how it is executed. A strong idea poorly executed will be much less profitable than an ordinary idea excellently executed.

Once you have an idea which you feel enthusiastic about going to the market with, before you commit your resources to it, it is necessary to validate it to find out the chances of its success in the market.

Here are a few questions you need to ask for this purpose:

☐ Is there a market for your idea? Is the number of potential customers large and growing? (I did not deal with the second question and that led to the closure of my first consulting venture.)

☐ Who is your customer and what is his or her specific problem that you plan to solve?

☐ How are these people currently solving their problem, that is, what is your competition? Is there a lot of competition?

☐ How much better or cheaper are you than your potential

customers' current solution, and can you maintain that advantage

☐ Does the market have money?

☐ Can you easily get the product or service to your customers?

☐ And, most importantly: are you and your team suited to this task - do you have the right knowledge and network in this industry? Are you passionate about the problem or industry? Do you know how to market and sell the product/service?

Subjecting your idea(s) to these tests will reveal to you whether your idea is a good business proposition. If not, you may have to tinker with it, supplement it with something more etc. to make it workable.

9. Planning Your Business

We plan everything. Many times we are not aware that we are planning. We plan even the smallest activity like brushing our teeth or wearing a shirt. The moment we decide to do it, we visualize how the process would be.

For small or routine activities the planning process is also very short and quick. Major activities like building a house or going on an overseas trip need more deliberate and detailed planning. And starting a business is a very major activity and therefore needs a lot more systematic and detailed planning.

Why is planning necessary?

Planning is necessary for several reasons.

Planning makes you aware of all aspects of the activity.

Planning makes you aware of several possibilities – favorable and unfavorable – and this helps you decide beforehand your possible responses to take benefit of the favorable developments, avoid unfavorable ones or mitigate the harshness caused by them.

Planning enables you to make a fair estimate of the time, money, and other resources required.

Planning enables you to prepare a step by step approach to implement the project, decide when to start various activities so that they are finished in time to take care of the dependencies.

Some activities are simple and can be planned informally. Like, say, buying a camera. But some activities are complex. They have various components that individually need to be performed, be in place, executed and so on. It is therefore necessary to plan for them formally and in detail.

Starting a business is a very major and complex activity. It needs several activities under several heads to be done meticulously. It is impossible to keep all of them in the head. It is impossible to make sure that they are delegated to the proper persons and their progress monitored and corrective measures taken in the absence of a written plan.

Strategic Planning

Strategy is some plan of action that is designed to give the planner an edge or an advantage over his opponent(s). it need not result in an absolute victory, but just a small lead, a small head start, over his opponent or competitor, like say a small first innings lead, or a single mark more than the topper. The advantage is that this small advantage places him a bit ahead of the competition, which he can capitalize upon to increase the lead. Repeated, this process can potentially result in an unbeatable lead in the market in due course. Microsoft, oracle etc. are good examples.

Historically strategy was used in statecraft and warfare.

In modern times, the same principles are used in business to gain advantage over the competition.

Principles of Strategic Planning

There are four basic principles of strategic planning. They are easier to understand but need a lot of thinking to work with. They are challenging and hence not only new entrepreneurs but a lot of well-established companies fear undertaking this exercise and take the easy way out.

But there are no shortcuts to success. Starting a new business absolutely needs strategic thinking, first for survival and then for gaining market leadership. So let's have a look at these principles.

Determine the result you want to achieve.

Absolute clarity about what you want to achieve through your business is absolutely essential, because that will decide all the future course of action.

Going to Antarctica needs different planning and preparation than climbing the Mount Everest. If doing a part-time side business is what is in your mind, the type of preparation and its scale will differ from what you will need to do if building a business that will see your next 3 – 4 generations through.

So spend a good amount of time on this issue.

What is your aim in starting this business?

Do you want to earn a decent living through your business?

Do you want financial stability through your business?

Do you want to pass on the business to your children as your legacy?

Do you want to expand your business to its maximum?

Satisfactorily dealing with these questions will show you the way ahead.

Identify the best methods to reach your goals.

Having established the goals you want to achieve, the next obvious step is to find out what the most effective ways of reaching those goals are. This search will be multi-pronged. You will brainstorm. You will search the Internet. You will talk to people. You will look for examples. You will undertake What if..' kind of exercise. You will look beyond your field, into other related or even totally unrelated fields for clues and ideas.

At this juncture, bagging as many ideas as possible is the goal and therefore you must not pass the ideas cropping up through the filters of cost, duration requirement of manpower, work involved, other people involved, complexity, long drawn legal procedures etc. That comes at a later stage. Eliminating ideas on these or any other criteria will kill creativity and fresh ideas will not come.

It is absolutely necessary to note all these ideas in a journal. It is impossible for us to remember all of them, and once they are lost, they are lost forever. Also when you are collecting ideas from various sources, you will want to keep proper notes of the source of the ideas, so that you can thank them later as also get back to them for further information etc. if necessary.

It is also necessary, as the next step in this quest, to mentally walk through all these options to visualize or have a feel of how the process would be and how the goal will be reached. I like this phase because it's kind of dreaming and therefore fun!

It is obvious that the more seriously this exercise is done the better will be the quantity as well as the quality of ideas you will harvest, and this means you will have many better options available to choose from.

Consider the constraints you face.

This phase expects you to look at your harvest from a different perspective. You are acutely (and sometimes painfully!) aware of your constraints and limitations.

You wish they were not there but they are and you can't wish them away. Your methods through your financial, political, social, manpower, time, scale of operations and all other constraints (personal likes and dislikes included) and see what remains.

If you are still left with a thick bunch of methods, pat yourself on the back for having done a good job in the previous step. If you're left only with an item or two, you will need to go back to the previous step and grab a few more candidates for scrutiny.

Adopt your methods to get the best results you can within those constraints.

This is pretty obvious and doesn't need much elaboration. Whatever methods remain as a result of the previous exercise, are available to you to choose from to implement and achieve your goals. But they will be generic and you will need to tailor them to fit your business.

But my preferred choice of working in this step and the previous one is different, what I do is I examine the ideas for their effectiveness and choose a few. I then examine what resources they would need. If there are any constraints, I try and work out how those constraints can be overcome, eliminated or avoided. So rather than dropping a potentially highly effective method because of constraints, I work on reducing the effect of the constraints so that I can still use that method. You are free to decide for yourself.

Use it.

Earlier I said there were four principles. So why this fifth one? This is because the story doesn't end with preparing that strategic planning document.

The first thing is that strategic planning is not a onetime exercise. It is repetitive. You will need to repeat it after you get your initial success with it to capitalise on it. You will need to repeat it when conditions change – internal, external, national, international, financial, social, political and what not. May be a major competitor has closed shop or may be a strong competitor is about to enter the field. In fact even before this phase, you may have to repeat it to get it right, in case you didn't get it right the first time or later found that you are not very happy with it.

Then, the most important thing is to USE it, to IMPLEMENT it.

Even the best of the plans, if not implemented devalue the paper on which they are written or printed. Remember that an ordinary plan, well-implemented, yields much more return on investment than an extraordinarily superb plan collecting dust on the book shelf.

Do it.

Go ahead and implement that plan.

Remember, you don't have to be good to get going, but you have to get going to be good.

10. The Business Plan Document

Having done the strategic planning, it now is the time to turn to the business planning document and using it for planning your business.

There are several versions and templates available on the Internet to compile a business plan (one good site is www.bplans.com. A number of templates and sample business plans are available. Check it out.) It doesn't matter which one you use so long as it makes you think of all facets of opening a business.

A business plan must have the following 3 essential elements.

1. Focus: You cannot do everything. You cannot solve every problem of every market. It is just impossible. You have therefore to eliminate much and focus on what you can do well and what you enjoy doing. Plans don't work when they try to include everyone and everything.

2. Specifics: Milestones, financials, timelines, ship by's, landmarks. A part of a business plan document deals with conceptual and high level thinking and planning. But there is a concrete part to the business plan document. It must go into detail and speak of what will happen when, who will do what, quarterly sales and profits, tracking, monitoring, analyzing and soon. They are what give teeth to the plan. These are essential to make sure that implementation is proceeding as planned and if not, take corrective measures.
3. Financials: This is very important. Since most of the entrepreneurs are technocrats, interested primarily (and usually solely) in the technical part of the product, the financial aspect of the business is neglected and the venture immediately becomes a strong candidate for failure. This is because selling for more than direct costs does not

equal profit. This is because sale is not money in the bank account. Many a profitable ventures go under because there is not enough cash to pay for supplies.

Paying attention to how cash is going to be available for the business how the operation-cycle will go and making your commitments accordingly is necessary. Secondly, your investors, you and your banker, all need to be convinced that this is a profit-making proposition.

Constructing a well balanced cash flow is necessary. In addition to the other things, it is highly educative.

The above three things are an absolute must in any business plan document. But there are several other things that it should contain to give the reader a fair idea of what all is combining to make this a business. These items also make it compulsory for the entrepreneur to think about them and make a statement about them – something, given a choice, he would not have done.

The other items that should find a place in the Business Plan Document in order to make it complete are:

The Executive Summary (should be compiled last, being a summary of the rest of the document)
Business Concept

It is an answer to questions like

☐ In what market does your business compete?

☐ What does your business do?

☐ What quality image will it have?

☐ In what price range will it compete?

☐ What volume of sales is expected?

☐ What customer needs are met?

☐ What makes it unique from the competition?

The Marketing Plan
(A summary of the separate marketing plan should be made here)

Management or Operations Plan

Strategic Plan

In the western world, a business plan is used for the purpose of obtaining finance from venture capitalists, banks etc.

To sum up, a business plan document is a very important document as far as a business is concerned. it must receive the same respect at the hands of the entrepreneur. It is a detailed document requiring a good amount of thinking and field work. It must be compiled with due care and after due research. Data, especially about the market and the competition must be filled up only after due field work. Compiling the financials is not very difficult, if you start visualising how your business will progress from month to month. This work should not be outsourced to an accountant although his help can be used.

The plan thus prepared will need to be modified in the context of the actual performance as well as the changing market and economic scenario. But the value of the business plan lies in the process of planning which is very educative and definitely stands to benefit the entrepreneur by giving him a more holistic idea of his business.I have briefly mentioned a Marketing Plan in the paragraphs above. The next chapter deals with it in more detail.

11. Marketing

I know this word does make a lot of you uncomfortable. It creates before your mind the picture of aggressive people almost lying about whatever they are marketing, assuring a hundred things which just aren't true. Im sure your experience about marketing and marketing people isn't exactly inspiring.

This is because many marketing people don't do it right, not because marketing is bad.

Marketing, in plain simple language, is getting people excited about you and your services or products so that they buy your services or products.

And how will people get excited? First they have to know what you and your products or services are. Then they may get interested enough to make further enquiries or research. Then, when they are thrilled with what you have to offer, they may get excited about it and buy it and tell others.

And who are the people who should know these things? Those who are likely have use for it. It's not very helpful if the people who know about you and your product or service are not going to need it. A diabetic, even if he knows a great deal about the delicious confectionary you make, has little use of it.

So, we have a working definition of marketing for our guidance.

Marketing is making relevant people getting excited about your product in the hope that they will buy, and tell others.

And how do you do this?

This you do by telling them about it. That is marketing.

Without your telling them, how are they going to know who you are, what you do, what is your offering (service or product), how good it is, where they can get it, whether they can try it out, whether they will have your support after the buy it and how it will be available, who else has used it etc, what if they don't like it and want to return it?

That is why shops have signboards.

That is why there are yellow pages.

That is why there are advertisements.

That is why there are business cards.

That is why there are websites and blogs and social sites.

That is why there are reviews in the newspapers.

So, in fact, marketing is educating your prospective customers about you and your products or services. And this also includes educating them about the conditions under which your product or services can be useful to them.

Does it sound bad?

A sale can happen in one of the two conditions – either you approach the customer and request him to buy, or she approaches you for a purchase. When you approach a prospective customer with a request to buy, you are at a disadvantage. The prospective customer has an upper hand. He can reject or he can make demands that you may not like. But when she approaches you, you are in a better position. By the time she approaches you, she has information about you and your product and thinks favourably about it. She is almost ready to buy it. Therefore the sale is easier. Not so when you approach her.

Marketing is what gives her the information to make a decision to approach you.

Marketing is what creates a favourable impression in her mind about your product or service. Marketing is what tilts the balance in your favour.

Marketing is what makes your task of selling that much easier. Will you be surprised if I tell you that we are always marketing ourselves? Yes,

ALWAYS. Whatever we do, whatever we say, or don't say conveys something about us to others and they make or modify their opinions about us, and take decisions based on those opinions. This should make us watchful about how we dress, walk, speak, present ourselves, present our case, handle various

situations and treat others. So the watchword here is —WATCH IT!‖It is not that you are new to marketing. You have done it before.

Remember that time when you wanted to be in that Cricket team and they were not sure? What did you do? Did you just give up? No, you told them what position you bat in but that you can fit anywhere. You told them about your being a very good fielder in the slips. You told them about your being a good off break bowler. You told them about where you played earlier.

What were you doing? You were marketing yourself, nothing else.

So, don't feel bad about marketing. Don't discount it. Don't underrate it. Don't run away from it. Don't be under the false impression that you don't need it.

Don't be under the impression that the market will somehow discover you and your product. Market doesn't have time, especially if someone else is right before their eyes. Howsoever excellent you or your product may be, you do.

Remember that a well-marketed average product sells more than an ill-marketed extraordinary product.

It is imperative that as a part of your preparations to open your own business,you think of how you will market your business.

It starts with the customer. In business, everything starts with the customer.

Who is your customer? Where is he? How are you going to contact him? What methods of contact does he like? How are you going to get him interested in you and your product or service? What message are you going to give him? These are only few of the questions that you need to raise and then answer. This is because your marketing, to be effective, has to have a focus. And this focus will only come by examining all components like the customer, the medium, the message, and also the budget. It is important to think through these issues so that the money is wisely spent and there is no wastage.

For a layman marketing is synonymous with advertising. It may be alright for a layman to think so, (it is not), but you as a business owner should know better.

Advertising is only one way of marketing, and a very ineffective, unfocussed and expensive it can only be effective when supplemented by other forms of marketing. So, when considering marketing of your business, don't immediately start thinking in terms of issuing a half-page advertisement in the Times or a national paper! It won't work.

There are hundreds of ways of marketing. You can choose one or several of them depending upon the market, budget, product, your own tastes and that of your target customer, and your creativity. The basic rule is that marketing is a communication directed towards the prospective customer to get him interested.

Any means of communication and anything that will get him interested is potentially good for marketing.

Marketing need not be expensive or very expensive. For example e-mail is a good medium for marketing and is quite inexpensive. A website is a medium of marketing and is not very expensive in terms of money and it lasts much longer.

On the other hand, newspaper advertisements are expensive, especially because one is not enough and you need to run a campaign.

In short, you need to identify a few methods of marketing that go well with your product or service, have a better chance of reaching your prospective customers, likely to be liked by them, effective in getting them interested in your product, and is within your budget.

Another part of marketing is that you need to do it consistently. Out of sight is out of mind is the rule and your product needs to stay before their eyes all the time. One-shot marketing is a bad idea. So you need to identify a few suitable methods of marketing and then keep repeating them.

It is very funny that probably the most powerful method of marketing your product or service that is available to you is not in your control! You can't start it. You can't stop it. You cannot moderate, channelize or modify it. You don't have to have a monetary budget for it. And you don't run it.

It is run by your thrilled customers by telling others, by talking about it. It can run anywhere, anytime, 24X7, through any means of communication. It is called word of the mouth publicity. Word of mouth publicity campaigns are run by highly satisfied and thrilled customers. They run them voluntarily expecting nothing in return.

They just talk about your product or service to others telling them how good it is and urging the others to try it out. It is very effective because the recommendation goes to the prospective user from a trusted source and someone who has actually used it or experienced it as opposed to from the producer or vendor, whom the prospective customer does not trust.

The investment in this type of marketing consists in creating highly satisfied and thrilled customers. Their experience with you must be so good that they feel compelled to talk to others about it, or write a letter to the editor about it, or an article reviewing it.

A marketing plan, like the business plan is a written document. There is no single master format universally used. This is because people's perspectives and points of view differ and so do market conditions and scale of operations. A number of formats are available and can be used. However, regardless of the format, they more or less contain all the information. The most important purpose that a marketing plan serves is to make the entrepreneur aware of what marketing is, what background information is required to prepare it, and how to prepare one.

The other equally important purpose it serves is that it compels you to think about various aspects of marketing and write about it. This compels you to have a clear idea of the matter to begin with. To have this clarity, you have to think. You have to research (not only on Google!), you have to move around in the market and collect information. You have to talk to people and ask questions. This activity brings you closer to the market and gives you a clearer picture. Then when you start writing it, the act of writing itself helps you clarify your ideas further.

The process of writing a marketing plan forces you, a technocrat, to deal withsuch aspects of your business as forecasts and lead generation and so on whichyou would not have paid attention to, but are crucial and critical to the success and profitability of your business.

You will have observed that there is already a section in the Business

Plan document which deals with your marketing arrangements. Then why is a separate document needed for the same purpose once again?

The reason is in the detail. In the Business Plan, marketing is not the main focus and is included as a summary. Whereas in the marketing plan, the main focus is marketing and is therefore dealt with in much more detail.

It is therefore prudent to first draft your marketing plan and then to summarise its contents in the Business Plan.

A good marketing plan document should deal with at least the following items:

The Mission Statement: Don't be stressed. A mission statement is nothing but an explicit statement of the overall objective(s) of your business.

The Target Market: This part defines the market that you are planning to serve in as much detail as possible. Also it will want you to list down your reasons for choosing that particular market.

Market Analysis: This is that part of the Marketing Plan where you will report everything you have researched or found about your target market. It goes into more details than the previous part and tries to quantify its attributes like its size, whether it is growing, shrinking or stagnant, how is it being served at

present, who the other players are, what is the gap, have previously efforts been made to solve this problem, and, if so, with what results, how is the target market managing at present, does it have the financial capacity to buy your product or service, does it know about this kind of product or service or will it have to be educated.

Raising and answering these questions leads to a lot of clarity not only about you market, but also about your product or service and pricing.

Objectives and Strategies: This part of the Marketing Plan is about documenting your objectives and then the strategies through which you hope to achieve those objectives.

The basic question is, —What do I want to achieve through my marketing initiatives?‖ Is it more customers? More leads? More subscribers to my blog or newsletter? More awareness? More visitors to my website? More number of downloads of my white paper or eBook?

Once the objective is clear, it becomes easier to develop strategies for achieving those objectives. It also makes your research easier, if you are not satisfied with your stock of strategies.

Sales Forecast: You need to prepare a forecast of sales for the next 12 months, month by month. You will do this taking a realistic view of the marketing efforts you plan to do, the current market conditions and competition, your manpower and other resources.

Your sales forecast will also depend on your own approach

Do you want to enter the market aggressively? – do you just want a small entry in the field to test the waters? – What portion of the market do you want to cover – Small? – Medium? – Large? It will also depend on the time it takes for the initiatives to bear fruits.

Alternatively you can turn the whole thing on its head. You can decide what results you want at the end of the period and work backwards to what initiatives you need to take and what and how much resources you need to deploy to achieve the results you've decided upon.

Implementation: This part of the Marketing Plan makes you go into the details.

Having listed what you propose to achieve, now you proceed to list how you will implement your chosen marketing methods to achieve those results.

It can be a calendar of when to do what.

It can also be a role-assignment sheet designating who is to do what and when. It could also be a reporting and coordinating structure.

How elaborate your implementation plan is will depend on how complex your operation is and how many teams or players are involved.

But when you're just starting out, in all probability, you will be the only person playing all the roles. Also, you may be working under a low budget for marketing.

Therefore choose wisely. Choose well. Give a lot of thought to how you will go about it. Use as many of the free and low cost channels available as possible.

Also don't opt for methods that are physically too taxing. Conserve energy. Get yourself a mentor or an advisor to guide you.

You will find a number of marketing plan templates on the Internet. Sample marketing plans are also available.
Note them down. And then write your own plan. Do not copy someone else's plan. Copying someone else's plan and using it is like treating yourself with medicines purchased on a prescription written for someone else.

One final word before we conclude. Don't start too many initiatives at a time. It would be strenuous and also difficult to gauge their efficiency. Start with one or two. Implement them with full preparation. Give them time to show results.

Measure their performance. Persist with whatever gives results.

Please bear in mind that execution is more important than planning. An ordinary plan well-executed will give better results than an excellent and sophisticated plan implemented half-heartedly.

It is only by trial and error that you will find out what works and what works best!

12. YOU

In a factory, there is machinery.

In a retail shop, there is commodity.

In a service shop, there is ....YOU.

In a factory, there is the entrepreneur.

In a retail shop, there is the shop keeper.

In a service shop, there is ....YOU.

And the machinery needs upkeep, maintenance, repairs.

And the shop needs cleaning, stocking and display to attract customers.

In a service shop, what do you need?

In a factory, there are maintenance people, repairers, engineers to keep the machinery fit and sunning.

In a retail shop, there are employees to keep it clean, suppliers to keep it well-stocked and their representatives to arrange the display.

In a service shop, there is ….YOU

I don't know whether you have realized it or not, but in a service shop YOU, the owner, are everything.

You are the means of production.

You are the reservoir of knowledge.

You are the service provider.

You are your most precious asset.

You are your company's most valuable capital.

Machinery and commodity can be replaced. Can you be?

What implications does this have?

Several.

You need to be fit. Always.

You need to be physically fit.

You need to be mentally fit.

You need to be technically fit.

You need to be financially fit.

You need to be emotionally fit.

You need to be socially fit.

You need to be …….. F. I. T.

Fitness needs discipline as the starting point. It also needs persistence. You will have to design ways to maintain your fitness under the various heads and then the discipline to follow it regularly and the persistence to keep doing it over a long, very long haul.

Physical fitness

Regularity in daily life is the starting point. As a student, you might be working or studying till late in the night.

Now, as the all-in-all of your service unit, you need adequate sleep at night so that you are and look fresh every day. You are permitted to look tired only in the evenings, not mornings. Your customers will notice. Also it is difficult to smile when you are tired. So, set up your routine accordingly. Sleep well.

Then you need to take adequate exercise. For two reasons. One, of course, is to remain fit. The other is, equally, if not more, important at your age is to look attractive. A well-in-shape muscular body impresses people even before you open your mouth or present your business card. It has a lot of impact on your influencing ability and this enhances your chances of winning the prospective client .And your hair style. When I used to have my hair on my forehead, my grandfather always used to say, —Hair grow on the head so that they should

remain on the head. If God wanted hair on the forehead, hair would have grown on the forehead.‖ Now that I am his age, I agree.

Keep them under discipline, on the head. Ladies, I know, will want to be excused from this prescription. But I think you too have got to adhere to this discipline. Listen, you are there not socializing. You are on duty. An office is a formal place and your work a serious business. You should keep it professional and matter of fact. Do not distract the attention of the client or your staff. So dress accordingly. Out of the office, you can wear whatever you like.

So, boys, if you are at the moment not very fit, start an exercise regime to build strength, stamina, and muscle. Discipline your hair to stay in order and on the head. Get used to wearing trousers and shirts and walk with your shoulders drawn back and chest out. See for yourself the jump in your confidence level.

Mental Fitness

You will need all the positives that you can get. You will need a strong positive attitude. You will need optimism. You will need a strong belief that things will turn out to be good. So on the one hand avoid company of pessimists and doubters. Avoid company of those who are satisfied with whatever little they have. Avoid company of those who try to drag you down. On the other hand seek optimistic people, those with positive attitude. Go to those who themselves

are perked up and make others so. This is very important. Studies of Olympic gold winners have shown that most of them expected to win, very few of them are such that thought they would not.

Another thing that should be done is to avoid reading pessimistic, depressing material, which in short means the newspaper and also the TV.

Read wholesome, good quality literature that will lift your spirits and awaken positive feelings in you. There are plenty of such books.

Technical health

Your aim is to succeed in your venture using your technical competence. For this you must constantly attract clientele. For this to happen, the fundamental requirement is that your technical competence must be of the highest degree.

You simply must be the best. Nobody should be able to challenge you on this point. For this to happen, realise that what you have learned in the college is not enough. In fact it may be outdated. Your branch of technology must have advanced considerably after the syllabus was set and the text books were written. So your first and foremost task, the first step in setting up your shop, is to update your knowledge.

That will boost your confidence. And make this a life-long habit, you will always need to stay ahead. If you do this, your reputation will spread so much and become so strong, that others will not dare enter your field and to that extent your competition will be less. You are all very intelligent people and it should not be difficult for you.

When you do this, you become an expert in your field. But how will people know that you are an expert? Show them. Show them through your work. Show them by writing in the local and national newspapers. Start a blog and write regularly.

Join associations and professional bodies of your discipline and become an active member. Your contribution will get noticed. Find opportunities to give speeches.

The suggestions are not exhaustive. You can and will find more ways of doing this as you go along and keep you antennas up.

You have plenty to do. So guard your time jealously. Avoid all time wasters. The TV is one major time waster. No watching BBC or Channel 4. I know it may hurt. But realize that all those people you see on the TV, the actors, the players and soon, have worked hard at fulfilling their dreams and that's why now people watch them – and pay for it. You and I have our dream yet to realize. That much sacrifice will be needed.

Then emails, Facebook and other such things. Don't get hooked to them.
You need emails for your business and personal matters. Keep it at that level. Don't check mails every half an hour. Study the pattern and decide upon a fair frequency in such a way that you also have chunks of time to do other things.

Remember, an email is the sender's priority. It need not become yours.

The Internet is also a potential time waster. No doubt it is a gold mine of information. But unless you are disciplined, you go on a clicking spree, surf a number of sites, read interesting (but useless) things and before you know, have lost two hours. Sounds familiar? So, protect yourself from aimless wandering.

Your mobile phone. Keep in mind that it is with you to facilitate your communication, to save your time, not to steal it. Use it wisely. Keep your talk short and to the point.

Friends can also be time wasters. While I shall never recommend ending friendships, slowly and gradually try and discipline them too.

Have confidence in yourself. If initially you don't have it, behave as if you have it. For this, I'll suggest an exercise. Sit down and on a piece of paper write down all things you did in your life so far, right from your childhood, which make you feel proud of yourself or make you feel happy about yourself. This will take some

time, maybe a day or two. Then prepare a fair copy, rearranging them if necessary. Read it out. How do you feel?

Now anytime you feel down, beaten, depressed, or unsure of yourself, read this paper. You'll be reminded of what you did. Then ask, —If I could do these, why can't I do this? What stops me? Who can stop me?‖ Then get up and do whatever you were feeling jittery about.

Another thing you should do is maintain a log of victories. Whenever you achieve something that stretches you, log it. And log it in detail. Record the issue, what was holding you back, how you overcame it, what you learnt about yourself in the process and why is this important for you. Reading this log once in a while will help you in many ways. It is small victories that give you the confidence and courage to face larger challenges. That is why they are important. Documenting them and your learning from them is important for this reason.

This —YOU‖ is the most important asset that you and your business has.

Take good care of it. You'll never regret it.

13. GOING FOR IT

This has been a long journey.

We started with our desire to earn a lot of money and become rich. I believe that middle-class boys and girls live their life torn between the desire to become rich to enjoy the pleasures of life, and an induced feeling of guilt about wanting to become rich. I very strongly believe that there is no need to feel guilty about wanting to be rich as it is neither illegal, nor immoral, nor anti-social, nor against the tenets of any religion nor unethical. In fact good, people must strive to become rich, because they will strive to earn their wealth through fair means, and as a result of serving the society. The money and wealth thus acquired will qualify to be called Lakshmi. Such wealth is earned with the consent and blessings of those who help create it, not out of force, coercion, fraud, deceit, loot or other illegal, unethical, or immoral means.

Thus I advocated that if you want to become rich, don't feel guilty about wanting to be rich. Feel happy or at least normal about it, and set about becoming so.

We then examined doing a job and doing business as possible ways of becoming rich and concluded that because of the tax structure, it is impossible to become rich doing a job. The laws are all made to protect the interest of the rich people as they can (and do) influence the rulers. They are never fair to the serving class or the middle class. Thus, _if you want to be rich, do your own business' is the conclusion we arrived at.

Then, assuming that you are convinced with my arguments, and that you are considering entrepreneurship as your preferred way of earning a livelihood, to help you choose a business or line of business, I discussed what kind of business has a better chance of surviving and prospering. We concluded that the more basic the need that your business proposes to satisfy or the more acute the pain or inconvenience that it proposes to relieve, the better are the chances of your business surviving and thriving. This is an important thing to keep in mind while making a choice.

Since I lay a strong stress on ethical and moral conduct of affairs, I then wanted to clarify to you my take on the moral obligation that every entrepreneur businessman has towards the society in which he is carrying on his business or profession. Your client or customer agrees to do business with you because he trusts you to be what you claim to be and do what you claim you can do to solve his problem. Your moral obligation is to do that. Why moral obligation? I say it is a moral obligation because many times it may not be a legal requirement and many times, even if it is, given the kind of legal system we have, the customer may not go to the court to enforce his right. He may bear the loss. But the injustice that he has met at your hand haunts you. It may or may not directly affect your business, but, you surely get a scolding form your conscience.

And that scolding is very pungent. So, better walk the straight and the narrow.

We are all educated people and do not do anything without being convinced about the need to do it – unless we are arm-twisted into doing it by our politicians or profiteering business community. So, while starting a business, it is necessary to clarify to ourselves our reasons for wanting to start a business. Our purpose could be to earn a decent living with a good living style of our choice. It could be to lay a foundation of a business that will outlive you and support your future generations, or it could simply be your way of fruitfully and gainfully spending your free time at the same time being useful to the society.

None of the reasons are better or worse than the other and all are fine. The reason why we should be aware of this is that our future decisions will be different if our purposes are different. It is therefore necessary to spend some time clarifying this to ourselves.

Having done this fundamental thinking and having given ourselves a strong conceptual foundation, we then jumped into examining our business idea. We are technically skilled people and believe that our skills are useful to the society, that the lives of the members of our society will be richer if they avail of our services. This prompts us to start our own service business. But there is a long way between an idea and a business. Is our idea practical? Is it commercially viable? Is it commercially viable on the scale on which I want to do it?
Does the society really need it? How long is it going to need it? Is the number of people in the society who may need this service large enough to make the trouble of starting a business worth it? Is their number growing? shrinking? Stagnant?

Who else is offering the same or similar services? Is he/she doing a profitable business?

Unless all these questions are satisfactorily answered, it would be dangerous to take the jump. We still have a few steps to go before we up the shutters.

Now assume that the business idea that we had in mind right from the beginning passes all the tests to make it a good, solid, profitable business opportunity and that your faith in it has grown to the level that you want to go ahead and start a business around it. Good! Great! Congratulations! But wait.

We just can't open a shop and start doing business from where we are right now. We need to plan it out properly. We have to make several arrangements before we up the shutters.

This phase is the business planning phase where we spoke about strategic planning to identify the result that we want to achieve, what the best ways are to get those results, what our constraints are and how to work within them.

I also proposed a contrarian approach starting with what I want to achieve, then going to what is the best way to achieve it, and to what does it take to implement this way and how can I make it happen.

Whichever way you follow, you need to make sure that your strategy is in place and you have devised a plan of action and are taking action on it. We also discussed the Business Plan document and how to use it. It calls for data and information on several issues about doing a successful business.

Compiling all this information may not be to our liking. Yet, for the sake of ensuring that all things have been properly taken care of, we need to subordinate our likes, dislikes, comforts and discomforts and compile them and interpret them diligently. The value of compiling a business plan is not in the plan itself, because the plan will never remain as you drafted it.

It will constantly change in response to the changing and unfolding of your business and the economy. The value of the business planning is in the process of planning. The various sources you tap, the various people you talk to, the data you collect, the time and energy you spend on making sense out of it all, trying to uncover patterns that could help you, the intensity that this process generates – to the extent that you start looking possessed – all are great teachers.

They teach you a lot about yourself, your market, your competition and the economy. While you are in it, it may be a torture, but still it is fun. And you come out a lot matured.

And finally we spoke about marketing. For a layman, marketing conjures up images and experiences of slick, sweet-talking deception-specialist men who make all false claims about what they are trying to make you buy and making promises about their great service and always being available for help and then, once that cash is in their pocket or the cheque is honoured by the bank, doing the famous vanishing trick. Sadly, the picture is quite accurate and would help any layman catch him, eyes closed. And therefore we equate marketing with deceit and lies.

But marketing is not that. Marketing is an activity aimed at educating the target market about your products or services to the extent that they get excited about it and consider buying it. If done ethically, it is an act that is beneficial to the target market because it introduces it to a superior product or service.

The common concept that people have about marketing is that of newspaper advertisements. This was largely true a few decades ago. But today, thanks to the Internet, a large number of channels, most of them free, and the others inexpensive are available for marketing activity.

A website, email accounts, Facebook, LinkedIn, YouTube and similar social platforms are very powerful media through which marketing can be done.

Like business planning, your marketing also needs to be planned and focused. Using a template to formulate your marketing plan is a prudent way to go about it. The best course of action is to select a couple of activities at a time and give them a fair trial and measure the effectiveness and to keep doing what works.

From the concrete, once again I went a step up and wrote about the most valuable asset that you have in doing anything in your life. That asset is YOU.

There I jotted a few points about what I feel your approach to yourself should be, if you want to succeed. I hope it makes sense to you and you feel prompted to take action on the suggestions made there.

Writing this book has helped clarify some of my ideas and organize them all in a proper way. The world of business is too big to be contained in such a small book, you will also agree. There's much more to it. So I have been jotting things I am leaving out of this book. It may all come out in the form of yet another book. Who knows?

Doing business is one of set of activities of life. Life and doing business have a lot of commonalities. One of them is the visibility available to us. In business, you cannot see much ahead in the future.

People complain about it. Accepted.

But so it is in life. How far ahead can you see with any degree of clarity? Not much. But you don't stop living life, do you? One makes plans to make it more predictable, safer, less risky, a little less full of surprises, considers contingencies and does something about them. He takes out insurance policies. He makes wills. He enters into forward contracts to pass on the risks.

But the uncertainty remains. It is the same with business. One takes all possible steps to mitigate risks and make the future at least somewhat predictable. But the risk remains.

After all doing business is a part of life and the properties of life are reflected in it.

Living a life or doing a business, both are like taking a walk in a garden which you have never visited. You do not know the territory nor the paths and pitfalls.

And it is early morning and there is a good fog around. The visibility is low. You can see only about 3 – 4 steps ahead. Beyond that you either see a white wall or very faint contours of some distant objects. You hesitate at the prospect of venturing out in such a climate. But you have to walk anyway.

As you start walking, your instincts to preserve yourself quickly sharpen. You suddenly become acutely aware of everything that is and that is happening

around. Your power of observation multiplies. You start noticing things you had never noticed – or seen - on clearer days.

You observe:

-At a time you can only see four steps ahead. But with every step that you take, you see one more step ahead. And you find it enough for you to plan your next step.

-You see a number of signposts and indications left for your benefit by those who have gone ahead of you. As they become visible to you, you easily avoid the dangers they wanted you to avoid. You thank them in your heart and move.

Those who went by this path were kind souls. They took the trouble of putting up warning signs. You can also hear some of them, who had gone ahead, guiding you to take safer paths!

-The path is not all that bumpy and rocky and treacherous as was made out by those who never set a foot in the garden. Oftentimes you were able to walk a good 200 – 250 meters without stumbling! Sometimes this is not possible on our city roads!

-After the initial tentativeness, you got used to the terrain rather quickly, to your own and everybody's surprise. In fact, you started liking the garden you were walking in.

-You have thus, become a successful entrepreneur, walking the path more confidently and also guiding others who would take courage from your example and step in.

So, keep walking. Enjoy. Experience the joy of doing something meaningful. Oh, and by the way, it's now time to GO FOR IT and do what you love the most!